This book belongs to:

D0324595

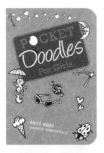

Collect Them All!

Available at bookstores or
directly from Gibbs Smith

1.800.835.4993

www.pocketdoodles.com

ANITA WOOD
DRAWINGS BY **CHRIS SABATINO**

GIBBS SMITH
TO ENRICH AND INSPIRE HUMANKIND

For John, my happy li'l camper.—AW

Manufactured in Altona, Manitoba, Canada in April
2013 by Friesens

First Edition
17 16 15 14 13   5 4

Text © 2013 Anita Wood
Illustrations © 2013 Chris Sabatino

Published by
Gibbs Smith
P.O. Box 667
Layton, Utah 84041

1.800.835.4993 orders
www.gibbs-smith.com

Designed by Melissa Dymock
Printed and bound in Canada

Gibbs Smith books are printed on either recycled, 100%
post-consumer waste, FSC-certified papers or on paper
produced from sustainable PEFC-certified forest/controlled
wood source. Learn more at www.pefc.org.

ISBN 13: 978-1-4236-3168-2

What's chasing Skyler and Zach out of this cave?

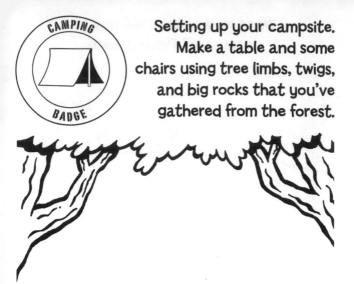

Setting up your campsite. Make a table and some chairs using tree limbs, twigs, and big rocks that you've gathered from the forest.

CAMPING BADGE

What kind of tent will you be sleeping in? Pitch it here.

Give this fire pit some roaring flames.

This bear found your food
supply hanging in the tree.
What is he dining on?

Fill the fishing creel with
your catch o' the day.

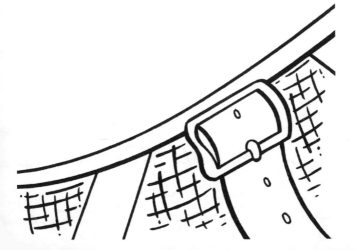

Who's taking this canoe for a paddle around Murtle Lake, British Columbia, Canada?

NATURE JOURNAL

Leave nature where you find it; draw or take a photo instead. Sketch the animal tracks you've discovered.

ANIMAL STUDY BADGE

ANIMAL TRACKS

CRAFTY CAMPER!

Making pet rocks. Draw
your new friend here.

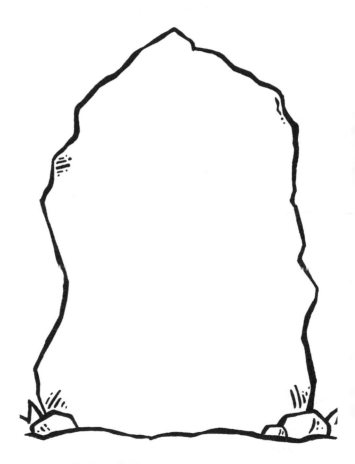

Hoot? Hoot? What's that you hear?
Close your eyes and see if you can
identify all the sounds around you (like
water in a stream, a croaking frog,
crickets, birds). Write or draw them here.

I want s'more!
Two graham crackers + chocolate
square + roasted marshmallow = YUM!
Build one here.

Your new hiking boots have left a huge blister on your big toe! Draw it.

Doodle a face on
this walking stick.

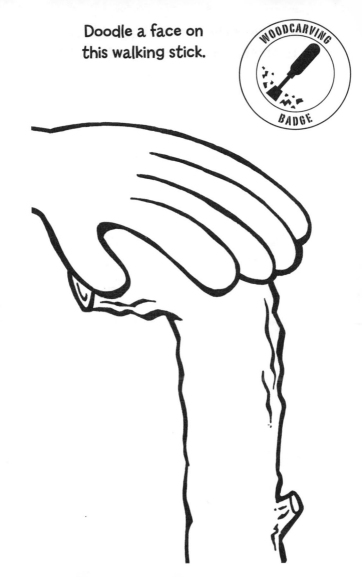

WOODCARVING
BADGE

Did you know that hummingbird babies
are so small they can fit in a thimble?
Draw one here.

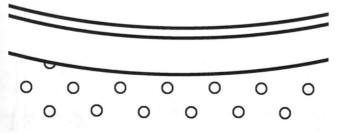

Design your family's camp banner.

Star gazing. Can you spot the big dipper (Ursa Major) and little dipper (Ursa Minor)? Draw them here.

What have you found in the nest?

The ants are marching away with your lunch! What are they carrying?

What's nibbling on your toes?

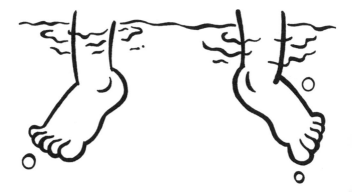

Did you know the Appalachian Trail is approximately 2,180 miles long and passes through 14 states, with trailheads in Georgia and Maine? Draw some of the friendly little mice you've found on the trail that have helped themselves to your sack lunch.

Buzz off! There's an annoying mosquito zinging in your ear. Draw it!

This little chipmunk is all set for winter!
Draw his stash of nuts.

What has this little forest bandit gotten into?

Give this flannel shirt a colorful checkered pattern.

Give Mr. Porcupine some quills!

Who's winning the tug-o'-war game?

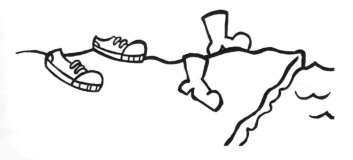

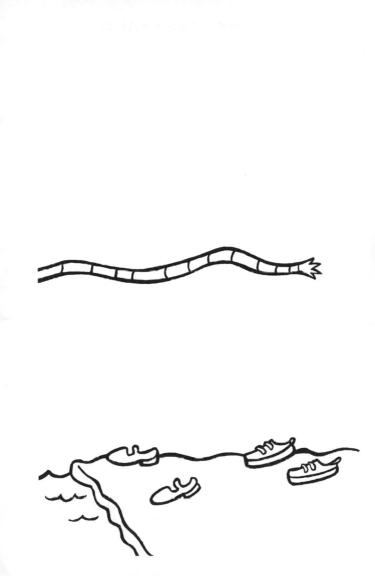

NATURE JOURNAL

Nature's sweet blooms. Draw some
of the wildflowers you've found.

WILD-
FLOWERS

What kind of creepy crawlers live inside this hollow log?

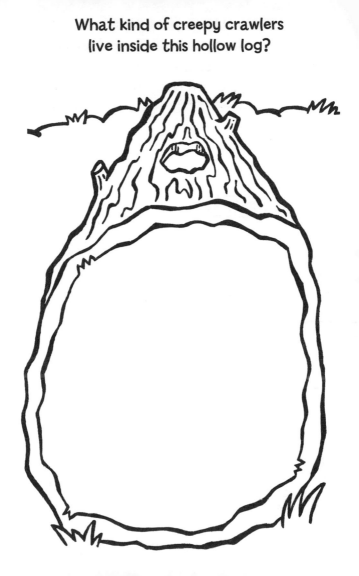

Did you know that squirrels accidentally plant millions of trees by burying the nuts they gather and then forgetting where they buried them?

Draw some places where Mr. Squirrel has stashed his nuts.

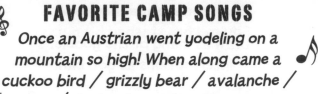

FAVORITE CAMP SONGS

Once an Austrian went yodeling on a mountain so high! When along came a cuckoo bird / grizzly bear / avalanche / cow / duck interrupting his cry. . . .

Draw as many of the yodeler's interruptions as you can!

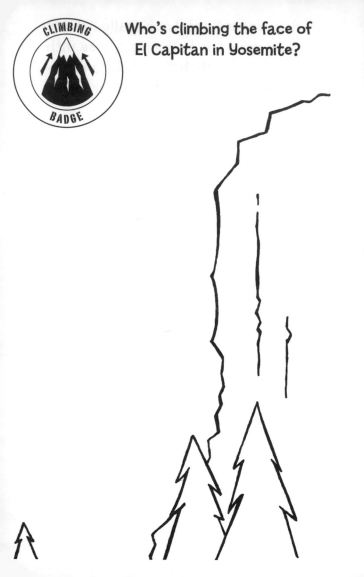

CLIMBING BADGE

Who's climbing the face of El Capitan in Yosemite?

Scavenger Hunt. Look really hard for and draw the following: a tree with blossoms, a Y-shaped twig, a moss-covered tree, and a clover leaf.

Something is lurking in the tree above. What is it?

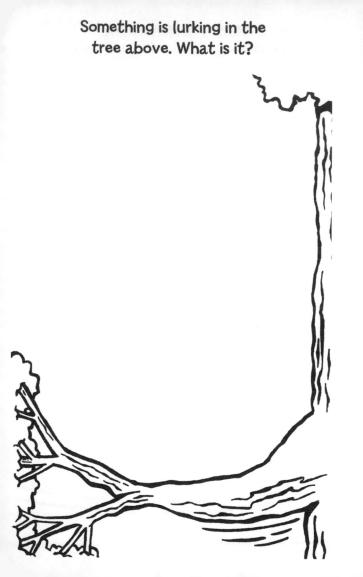

Gone huckleberrying.
Fill the bucket with the day's pickings.

CRAFTY CAMPER!

Draw a sign that warns campers about feeding the wild animals.

Help Bucky Beaver finish building his home.

Give these hiking boots a fun tread pattern.

What is peeking out at you from its hiding place in the tree hollow?

What are you studying under the magnifying glass?

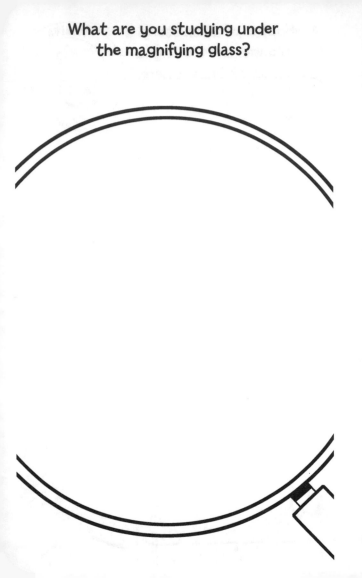

A whopper of a fish story! How big was the trout you just caught? Draw it here.

FISHING BADGE

These kayakers are headed toward
a waterfall. Draw their kayak.

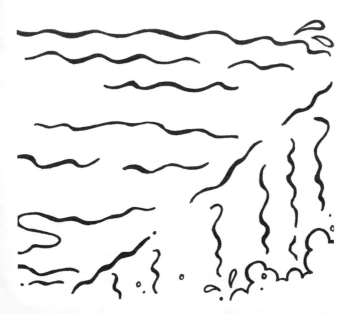

CRAFTY CAMPER!

Turn this paper bowl into a turtle.

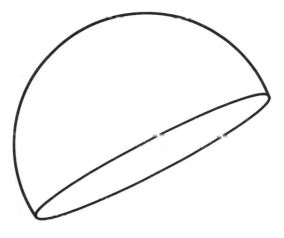

Toasting marshmallows! Do you like them lightly browned or completely burned? Add some to the stick.

NATURE JOURNAL

Compare leaves from different trees.

LEAVES

You've just met a crazy old prospector down by the creek. Draw the gold nuggets he's found.

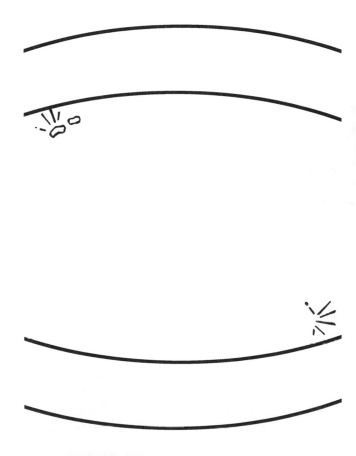

Pack up this donkey with
your camping supplies.

Where do these snowshoe prints lead?

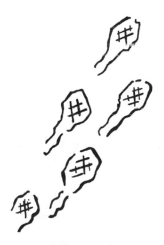

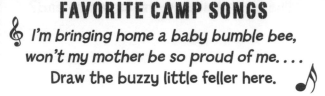

FAVORITE CAMP SONGS

*I'm bringing home a baby bumble bee,
won't my mother be so proud of me. . . .
Draw the buzzy little feller here.*

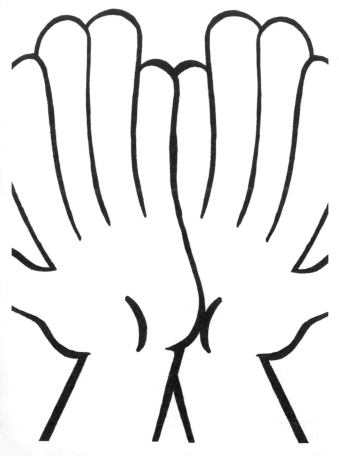

Finish building the log cabin.

a-Mazing! Find your way to the outhouse.

What's for breakfast?

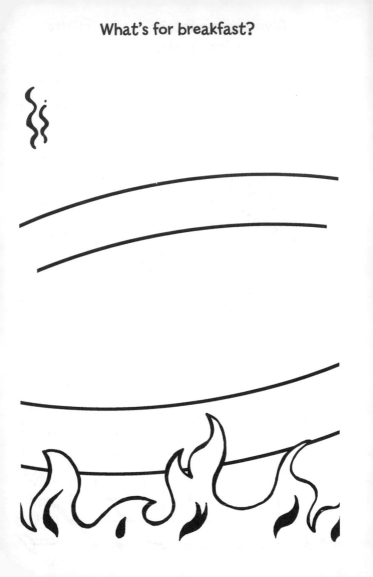

Give this mountain biker a fancy ride.

Camping bingo. How many of these things can you spot?

Did you know the Perseid meteor showers take place each year from mid-July to mid-August? Fill the sky with these tiny luminous particles.

This chameleon has taken on
the look of his surroundings.
What does he look like?

Finish drawing all the nifty
tools that fold up into this
super-mega-pocket knife!

Don't forget your long johns! What else did you pack in your backpack?

BACKPACKING BADGE

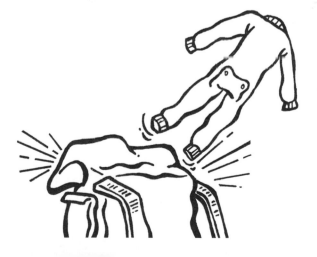

FAVORITE CAMP SONGS

Catalina Matalina, roomba-side, a wobble-side, a hoka-poka-moka was her name! She had two hairs in the middle of her head, gosh darn things were carrot red. Two eyes I wished to see, one looked at you and the other looked at me. Two teeth in the middle of her mouth, one pointed north and the other pointed south.

Draw poor Catalina Matalina!

What kinds of critters are swimming around this pond?

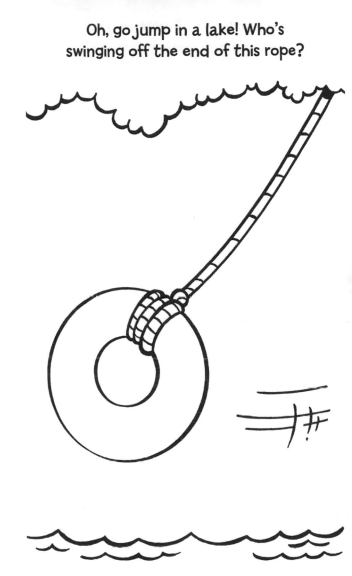

Oh, go jump in a lake! Who's swinging off the end of this rope?

Hot dog! Fill the bun and pile on your favorite toppings.

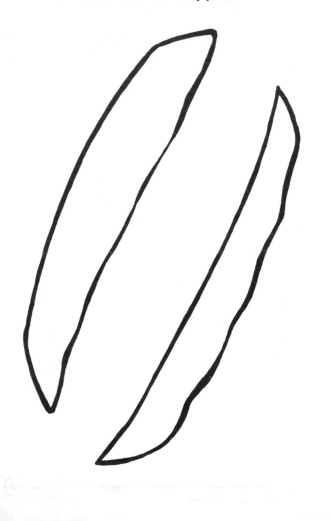

NATURE JOURNAL

Draw a spiderweb.

SPIDER-
WEB

STORYTELLING
BADGE

Finish writing a spooky story to tell around the campfire. Try to use all the following words: creaky, cold, damp, nightmare, thud, scratch, shadow, scream, hairy, slimy.

NO Swimming Allowed! There's a giant creature that lives in the lake! Draw it.

Sleeping in style!
Design the ultimate sleeping bag.

Did you know that a large group
of caterpillars is called an "army"?
Draw an army of caterpillars here.

Draw a scary "flashlight face"—
the kind you have when you're
telling ghost stories.

Legend has it that the Timbuktuian jelly bean bird migrates every year to select camping spots, and you've just seen it. She has pink and purple feathers, a bright orange beak, and lays jelly beans! Draw her.

CRAFTY CAMPER!

Add some pine boughs and pinecones to this picture frame.

ART
BADGE

Draw Mr. Toad's tongue to
help him catch his supper.

This poor camper stumbled
into a patch of poison ivy.

🎼 FAVORITE CAMP SONGS

There's a hole in the bottom of the sea.
There's a hole in the bottom of the sea.
There's a hole, there's a hole, there's a
hole in the bottom of the sea!
There's a log in the hole, a bump on the
log, a frog on the bump, a wart on the
frog, a fly on the wart, a flea on the fly.

Draw the log, and everything on it!

What kinds of items
will you find in this
first aid kit?

Alphabet hiking. Try to spot
something that starts with each
letter of the alphabet. Write
the word after each letter.

A _____

B _____

C _____

D _____

E _____

F _____

G _____

H _____

I _____

J _____

K _____

L _____

M _____

N _____

O _____

P _____

Q _____

R _____

S _____

T _____

U _____

V _____

W _____

X _____

y _____

Z _____

Scavenger Hunt. Keep your eyes peeled for the following items and draw: dew on a flower or leaf, acorns or other nuts, a fern, and a mud puddle.

How much wood did this woodchuck chuck?

Answer: He didn't give a hoot!

Why did the owl go "tweet, tweet"? Draw Mr. Owl.

Give this tent some camouflage
so that it blends in with your
camp surroundings.

NATURE JOURNAL

How many different types of pinecones
can you find? Draw each one.

PINECONES

Ahhh . . . the camping life's for me! String a hammock between these two trees.

Who's winning the sack race?

Warning! Did you know that before a spotted skunk is about to spray, it will do a couple of handstands? Draw the little guy in action.

Did you know that rabbits are herbivores, which means "plant eaters"? Give this little bunny a bunch of plants and veggies to nibble on.

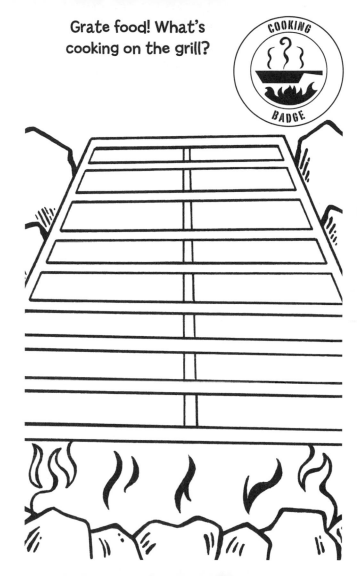

Grate food! What's cooking on the grill?

COOKING
BADGE

Have you ever heard about the legendary Bigfoot, or Sasquatch? What do you think it looks like?

Happenings in the hive! Draw
all the little worker bees and
her majesty, the queen!

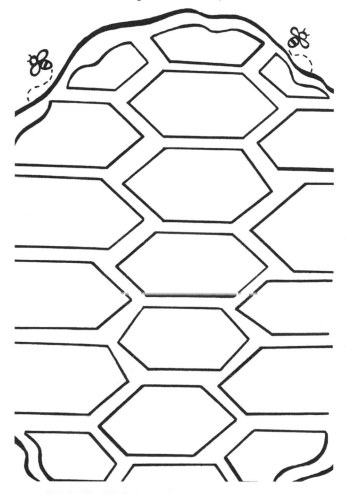

Phew! If these socks could only talk, what would they say?

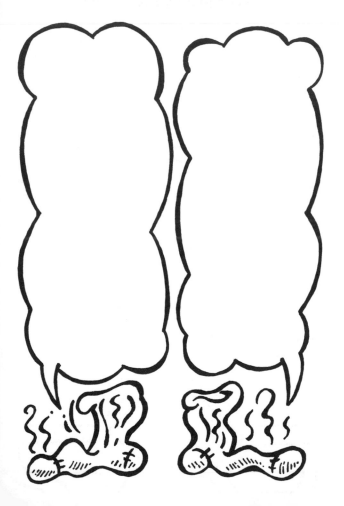

Guitar Lake, located on the John Muir Trail in California, is shaped like a guitar. Draw it.

FAVORITE CAMP SONGS

John Jacob Jingleheimer-Schmidt, his name is my name, too. Whenever we go out, the people always shout, there goes John Jacob Jingleheimer-Schmidt. La la la la la la la la!

Draw John Jacob!

Home away from home.
Design the ultimate camping RV.

Pack it out and leave no trace!
How many trash items have you
found? List or draw them here.

You've just wandered into an
enchanted forest where the trees talk.
Give each of these a funny face.

NATURE JOURNAL

Look for and draw some different
animal nests. Can you tell
what they are made of?

ANIMAL
NESTS

The trail you're hiking on ended at a cliff with a raging river below. Draw a bridge to get you to the other side.

White-water rafting down
the Colorado River.
Draw your raft.

Fill this jar with some lightning bugs you've caught.

Did you know that black bears are afraid of cats? They'll climb a tree to get away. Draw a frightened old bear and the cute little kitty that has him treed!

Draw an interesting leaf you've found.

Draw a waterfall flowing over these rocks.

CRAFTY CAMPER!

Turn this old egg carton into a
dozen cute little ladybugs!

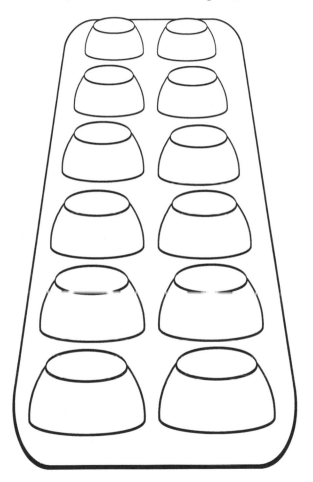

Trailblazing!

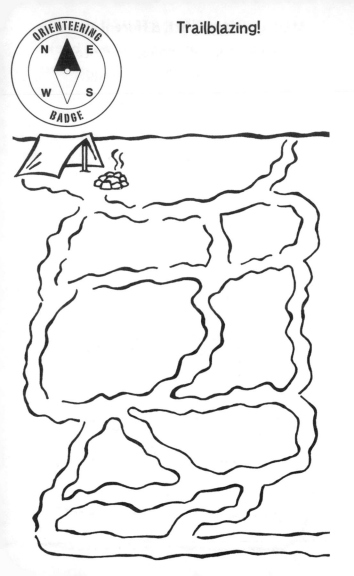

Mark your trail with different items so
you'll be sure to find your way back.

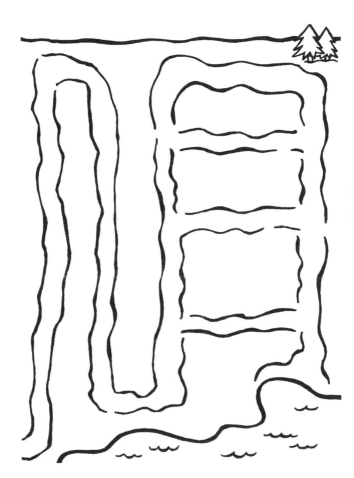

Close your eyes and take a deep
breath. What are some of your
favorite camping smells?

Speaking of smells, a small group of four-legged friends have just wandered into camp—and they aren't a family of striped cats! Draw mama skunk's kits!

Scavenger Hunt. See if you can find and draw the following: a leaf with insect holes, a ladybug, an animal hole in the ground, and a deer.

What kind of fishing goodies will you find inside this tackle box?

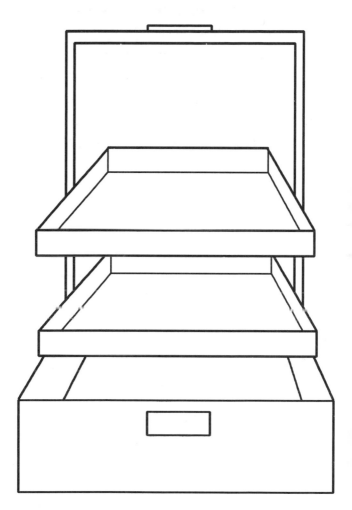

🎼 FAVORITE CAMP SONGS

There was a cow down on the farm
Moo, Moo, Moo, Moo, Moo, Moo
She gave fresh milk without alarm
Moo, Moo, Moo, Moo, Moo, Moo
One day she drank from a frozen stream
Moo, Moo, Moo, Moo, Moo, Moo
Now she gives up ice cream!
Moo, Moo, Moo, Moo, Moo, Moo, Moo

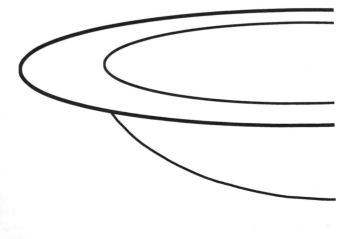

Fill this bowl with your favorite ice cream and toppings.

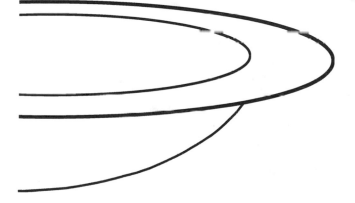

Deck this hat out with some
fancy fishing lures.

Did you know that a mosquito has 47 teeth? Ouch! Give this annoying pest his teeth.

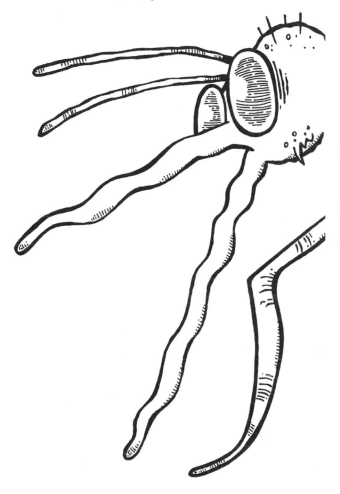

Who's filling up these hip waders?

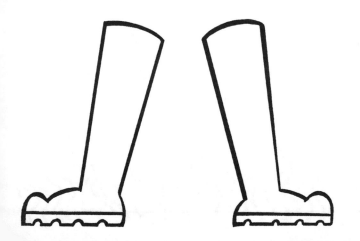

Somebody dropped a bunch of
popcorn kernels in the campfire
and now there's popcorn popping
everywhere! Fill the page with popcorn.

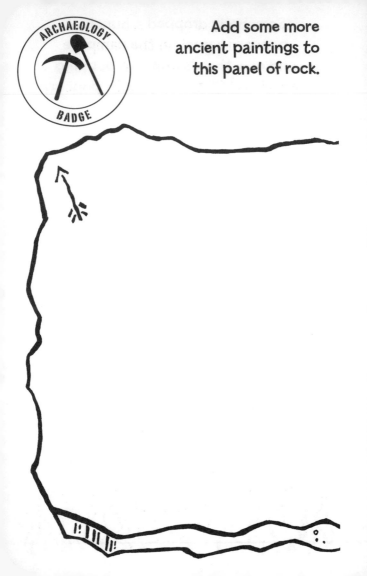

ARCHAEOLOGY
BADGE

Add some more
ancient paintings to
this panel of rock.

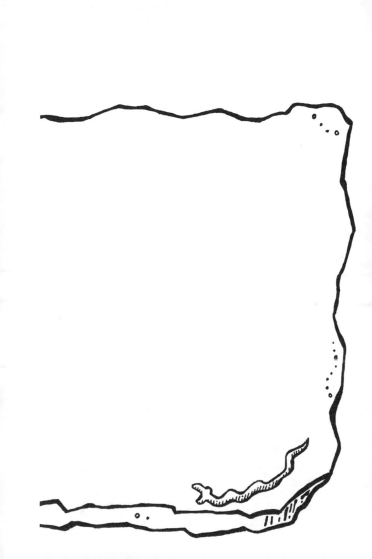

NATURE JOURNAL

My seashell collection.

Forest fairies are everywhere! They hide under leaves and behind toadstools. Can you draw one?

It's Take a Hike Day in Terra Nova National Park, Newfoundland, Canada.

What will these hikers find along the trail?

Grrr . . . You just found an old
grizzly bear claw. Draw it.

Fill this "Bug Hut" with as many different pests as you can think of.

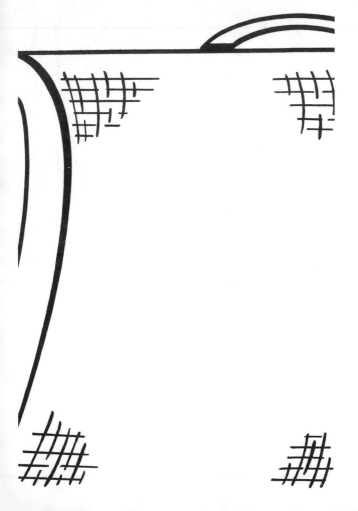

You're getting ready for a day hike. What kind of snacks are you going to pack in your knapsack?

HIKING
BADGE

Never go anywhere alone.
Who's your camping buddy?

Did you know that female butterflies
can taste things with their feet?
What is this butterfly dining on?

🎼 FAVORITE CAMP SONGS

Little Bunny Foo-Foo, hopping through the forest, scooping up the field mice, and bopping them on the head! 🎵

Draw this silly rabbit.

It's a bird! It's a plane! No, it's a flying squirrel! Connect the dots so that he can glide through the forest.

Help R. J. and Brittany get to the top
of Heavenly Ski Resort at Lake Tahoe,
Nevada, by finishing the gondola.

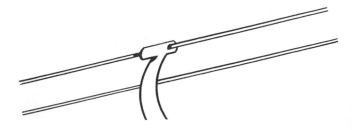

Dinner time! What's simmering inside the Dutch oven?

CRAFTY CAMPER!

Finish adding the web to this dream catcher. Don't forget to include some feathers and beads.

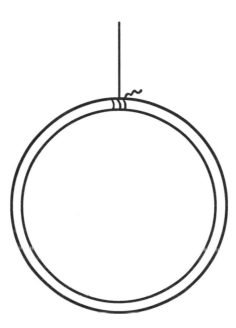

Who's coming down the zip line?
Are they happily excited, or
scared out of their minds?

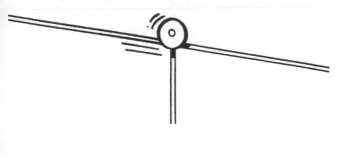

Dog sledding in Banff National Park, Alberta, Canada. Give these doggies a sled.

Reelin' in the big one, but it's not a fish! What's caught on your hook?

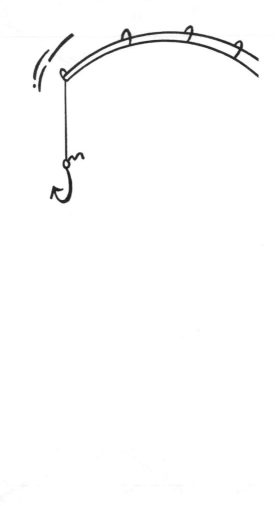

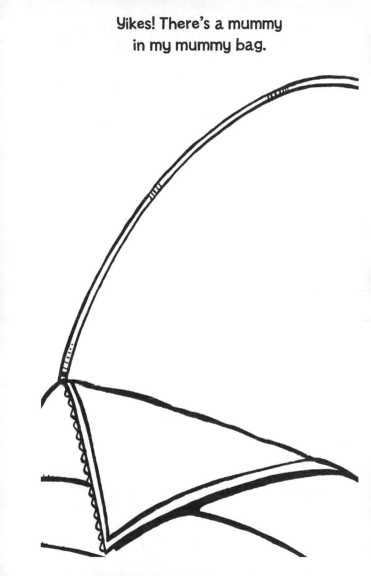

Yikes! There's a mummy
in my mummy bag.

NATURE JOURNAL

Do you know the life cycle of a butterfly? See if you can find some eggs on a leaf, a caterpillar, a cocoon or chrysalis, and a butterfly. Draw each one here.

BUTTERFLY

What did the beaver say to the tree?
Draw Mr. Beaver at work on this tree.

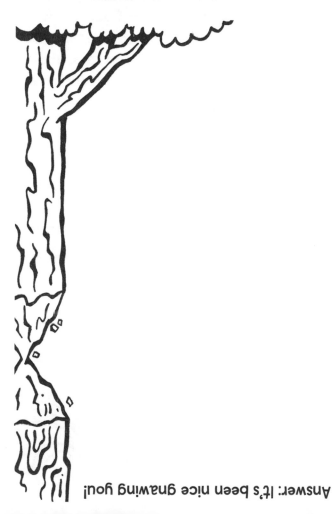

Answer: It's been nice gnawing you!

Kody loves four-wheeling.
Hook him up with a ride.

There's a storm a-brewin'! Fill the sky with thunderclouds and lightning bolts.

Scavenger Hunt. Keep a watchful eye out for: a bug that flies, a bug that walks, and something that slithers or wiggles. Draw each one.

Yum! Hobo dinners for supper. Add some potatoes, carrots, hamburger, and anything else that sounds good, to this foil pouch.

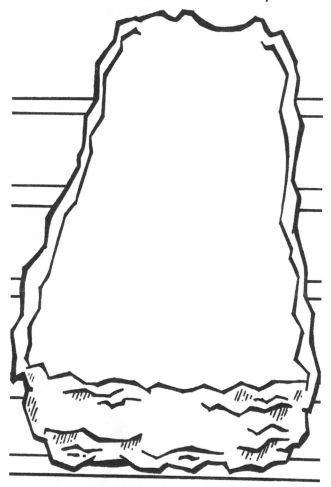

Give this old, mangy moose a
nice big rack of antlers.

Did you know that a "hoodoo" is a tall spire of rock, often with a cap or boulder resting on top? You can see tons of them at Bryce Canyon National Park in Utah. Draw some more hoodoos.

Baby Critter Match. Draw a line matching each mom with her baby, then draw them.

Spider

Bear

Frog

Deer

Owl

Wolf

Fawn

Owlet

Pup

Spiderling

Tadpole

Cub

FAVORITE CAMP SONGS

Five little ducks went out to play,
over the hill and far away.
Mother duck said, "quack, quack, quack,"
but only four little ducks came waddling back.

Draw these five naughty little ducks.

Summer's here and you're headed to Lake Powell in southern Utah. Draw the houseboat you'll be camping on.

This water-skier needs some skis and a rope to hang onto.

While boating on Lake Powell, you are lucky enough to see Rainbow Bridge, which is 275 feet wide and 290 feet high. It is considered sacred to the Navajo culture. Can you draw it?

Winter wonderland. Build yourself
an ice cave or igloo so you'll
have a place to keep warm.

Give this hotdogger a set of skis.

Cold comfort on Cold Lake in Alberta, Canada. Build your ice-fishing hut here.

NATURE JOURNAL

Quit bugging me!
How many different
insects can you find?

INSECT STUDY BADGE

INSECTS

Let's go camping, Hawaiian style!
Give this guy (*kane* in Hawaiian)
a surfboard and some waves.

Did you know that jellyfish aren't actually fish? They are shaped like an umbrella, and can be as big as a human or as small as a pinhead. Fill this tide pool with some "jellies."

This little gal (*wahine* in Hawaiian) needs a pretty lei around her neck.

Decorate this plain old shirt with some flowers or other designs so you'll fit in with the other tourists and campers in Hawaii.

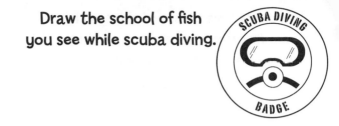

Draw the school of fish
you see while scuba diving.

SCUBA DIVING
BADGE

What kind of tree can you fit
into your hand? Add several
to this beach campsite.

There's nothing prettier than a
sunset while camping on the beach.
Draw one here.

What does the beach hut look like that you've been camping in?

Scavenger Hunt. Do some beachcombing and look for: a starfish, seaweed, driftwood, sea glass, and seabirds. Draw what you find.

Anyone up for a
game of volleyball?
Add some players.

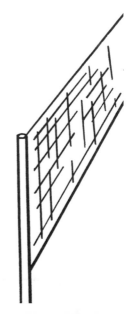

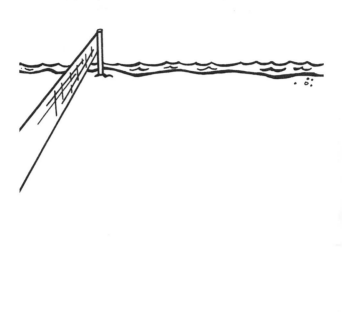

FAVORITE CAMP SONGS

*Kookaburra sits in the old gum tree,
eating all the gumdrops he can see....*

Draw the kooky kookaburra here
and give it some more gumdrops.

Watching the dolphins play. Fill the page with these happy swimmers.

Mini-menaces and no-see-ums. Ticks, chiggers, and fleas, oh my! This poor camper's covered with 'em. Draw the little pests.

Outfit this dirt bike with paddle tires for some serious sand shredding at Little Sahara, Utah. Make sure to attach a whip flag so people can see you coming!

Camping Word Search. Find all the words listed below. (There's a hidden message, too. See if you can find it!)

```
f  w  l  s  n  o  d  v  x  l  p  s
g  c  a  m  p  f  i  r  e  t  k  s
a  a  n  o  s  i  e  k  i  h  y  a
b  n  t  r  p  s  a  c  m  a  m  p
g  t  e  e  a  h  g  a  r  g  n  m
n  e  r  s  d  i  l  p  t  n  u  o
i  e  n  e  t  n  s  k  a  i  f  c
p  n  e  n  t  g  b  c  c  m  e  t
e  r  e  v  u  p  e  a  k  m  v  r
e  t  r  b  q  o  a  b  l  i  a  a
l  t  a  o  b  l  r  s  e  w  h  i
s  e  e  r  t  e  n  i  p  s  l  l
```

campfire	backpack	boat
lantern	sleeping bag	pine tree
deer	tent	bear
fishing pole	hike	smores
tackle	canteen	compass
swimming	bug spray	trail

Did you know that when the pioneers headed west, many of them brought all their belongings and supplies in handcarts. Some pushed and some pulled.

Give these trekkers a handcart.

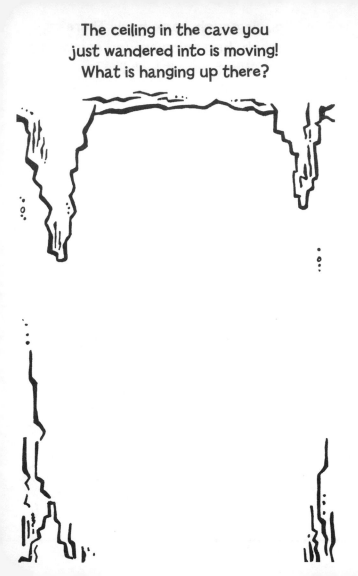

Cough, cough, hack, hack! There's a nasty bug going around camp. What does it look like?

NATURE JOURNAL

Can you say "ornithologist"?
(That's a big word for
someone who studies birds!)
How many different types
of birds can you spot?

BIRD STUDY

BADGE

BIRDS

Brrrrr! How cold was it when you got up this morning?

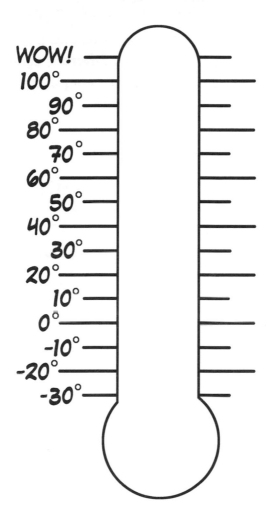

Greetings from Camp Wherever. Write a letter to your family telling them about all the fun things you're doing.

A LITTLE NOTE FROM CAMP wherever!

There's a _____
in my tent! Draw it.

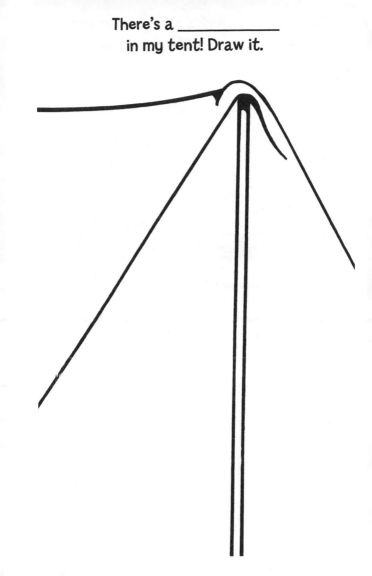

Give this anxious swimmer
a life preserver.

Whoops! You slipped in the creek
while crossing it. Draw your clothes
drying on the clothesline.

Scavenger Hunt. You're looking for: a rock with lots of colors, a beetle, a feather, a dandelion, and a blade of grass. Draw each one.

Set up an outdoor shower in this tree using the water jug you packed in.

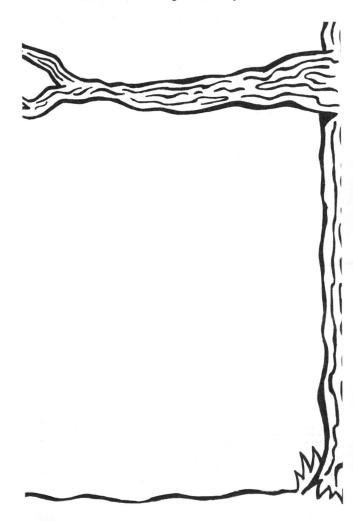

FAVORITE CAMP SONGS

*Oh, I had a little chickie and
she wouldn't lay an egg,
so I poured boiling water up
and down her leg.
My little chickie squawked
and my little chickie begged,
and so my little chickie laid
a hard-boiled egg.*

Draw your little chickie and
give her some colored eggs.

This spelunker (cave explorer) is getting ready to check out Wind Cave in South Dakota. Equip him with a hat and head lantern so he can see where he's going.

Crafty Camper. Draw a poster that reminds everyone to be careful with their campfires.

Draw a map of your campsite, including any landmarks that are around, like a stream, trail, etc.

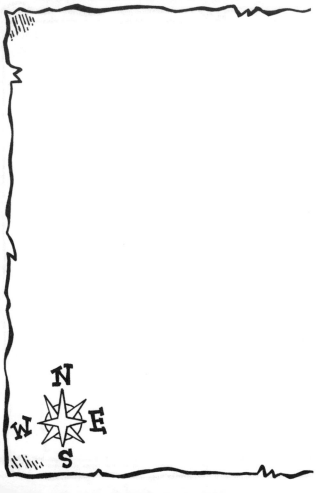

N
W E
S

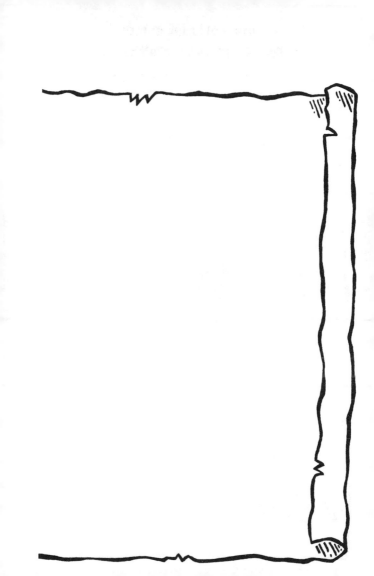

Where am I? Fill in the points of this compass.

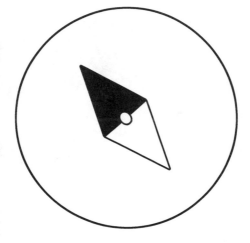

The lake you want to camp at is only accessible by floatplane. Add some puffy floats to this plane so you'll have a nice, smooth landing.

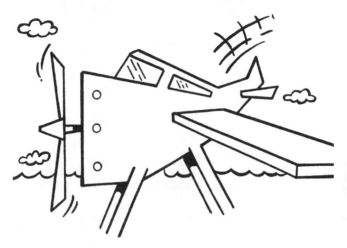

Something is pecking noisily away
at a nearby tree. What is it?

Let's celebrate Christmas in July!
Decorate these trees.

Nothing like a nice, hot cup of cocoa before sack time! Fill this mug with your favorite flavor and add some mini-marshmallows.

Devyn is out to win first prize in archery. Give him a bow and help him shoot some arrows into the bull's-eye.

ARCHERY BADGE

The overhand knot looks
like a pretzel. Practice
doodling a few here.

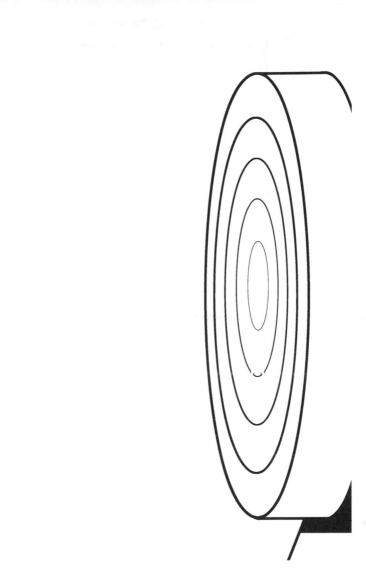

What was under your sleeping bag that kept you tossing and turning all night long?

NATURE JOURNAL

There are many different types of pine trees. How many can you find? Draw their different-shaped needles here.

PINE TREES

There's a full moon out tonight. Can you see the man in the moon, or does it look like cheese? Draw it.

Yum! What's roasting on the spit?

Shipwreck diving off the shores of Lake Superior, Michigan. What interesting things do you find?

Who's taking a nice soak in
Mr. Bubbles hot springs in
Yellowstone National Park?

Hiking along the Wonderland Trail in Mount Rainier National Park in Washington State, you spot a white rabbit carrying a pocket watch. Curious! Draw the hurried little fellow.

It's fall in Acadia National Park, Maine.
Draw the beautiful autumn colors
you see popping out on the trees.

FAVORITE CAMP SONGS

The littlest worm I ever saw,
was stuck inside my soda straw.
He said to me don't take a sip,
for if you do I'll surely slip.

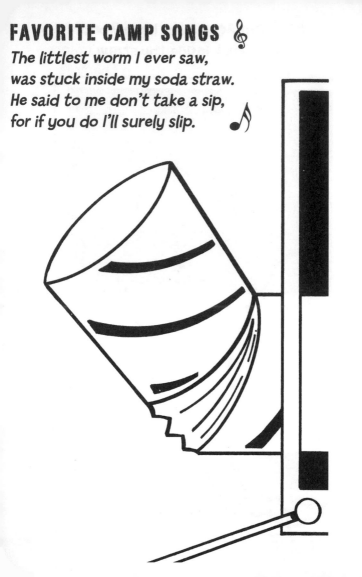

Draw this poor little worm
stuck inside the straw.

X~RAY

MUSIC BADGE

Write the words to your own fun camp song.

What's hidden inside the cave you've found behind the waterfall?

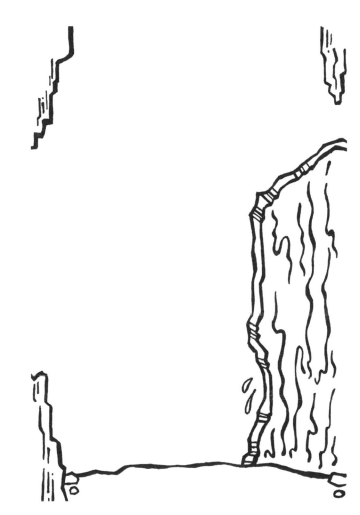

Breakfast is ready! Serving up the best pancakes you ever flapped a lip over! Stack 'em here.

Yikes! Somebody got caught
in their own snare!

Give each of these animals a set of horns.

Mountain Goat

Pronghorn Antelope

Bison

Elk

Bighorn Sheep

Mule Deer

Scavenger Hunt. You're in the desert. See if you can spot: a cactus, a lizard, a snake's discarded skin, a blooming cactus, and animal prints.

Dylan and Dalton are all set to do
some camping in their tree house,
except they don't have one!
Help them build one here.

There are lots of tools and equipment that are necessary for a successful camping experience, like a shovel. Can you draw a few more?

Camping at the Fort Bridger
Rendezvous in Wyoming. Decorate
the outside of your teepee.

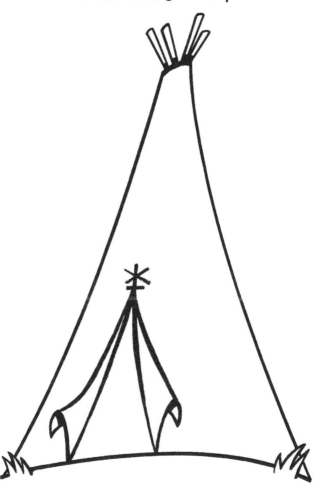

Did you know that a mole can dig
a 300-foot tunnel in one night?
Help Mr. Mole dig his tunnel.

Backyard camping with your friends.
Using a clothesline, set up your tent.

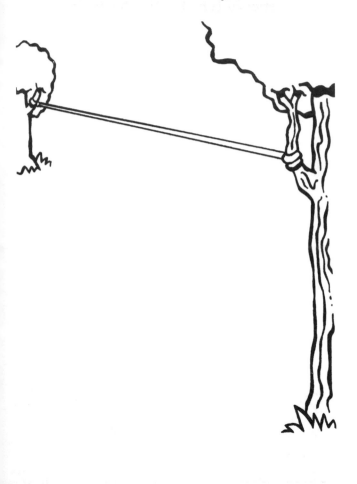

A delicate, stinky subject! Setting up the camp potty. Create a special tent for this purpose.

What are they catching in Pickle Lake, Ontario, Canada?

How many Doodle Badges did you earn?
Did you notice the different
Doodle Badges in the top corners
of some of the pages? Check off
below all the pages you finished.

- ❏ Animal study
- ❏ Archaeology
- ❏ Archery
- ❏ Astronomy
- ❏ Art
- ❏ Athletics
- ❏ Backpacking
- ❏ Bird study
- ❏ Camping
- ❏ Climbing
- ❏ Cooking
- ❏ Cycling
- ❏ First aid
- ❏ Fishing

- ❏ Hiking
- ❏ Insect study
- ❏ Knot tying
- ❏ Music
- ❏ Orienteering
- ❏ Scuba diving
- ❏ Snow sports
- ❏ Spelunking
- ❏ Storytelling
- ❏ Swimming
- ❏ Waterskiing
- ❏ Weather
- ❏ White-water
- ❏ Woodcarving